# braai & potjie
## flavours and traditions

JACANA

# Contents

Introduction — 15
Early days — 16
Braai — 21
Across the ages — 21
A day to celebrate — 23
It's a cultural thing — 24
The evolution of the traditional braai — 28
Fuel for thought — 32
Enter the braai master — 35
Essential tools — 36
It's all in the technique — 39
Cooking times — 42
Braaing dos and don'ts — 47
What do we braai? — 48
Potjiekos — 65
Introducing the three-legged pot — 65
Dos and don'ts of potjies — 70
Fish and seafood — 73
Saltwater fishing today — 81
Hunting and venison — 95
Variations on the theme — 103
Conclusion — 106

Recipes — 109
Baked camembert — 110
Braai broodjies — 113
Breakfast in a pan — 115
Broccoli, leek and bacon salad — 116
Butternut on the coals — 119
Cape salmon in vine leaves — 120

Citrus angelfish on the braai 122
Curried green beans 125
Curried pork-neck sosaties 127
Dessert jaffels 129
Flambéed plums 130
Four-cheese pap bake 133
Garlic-and-herb potbrood 135
Hamburgers 136
Honey-and-mustard chicken thighs 139
Mango, fennel and lobster salad 140
Marinated springbok 143
Marrow bones 144
Mealie bread in a can 147
Mealies on the coals 149
Mushroom risotto 150
Old-fashioned potato salad 153
Oxtail-and-orange potjie 155
Pizza with red onion, parsley and Parmesan 156
Pork trotters and beer potjie 159
Potato gratin in a pot 160
Quince jelly 163
Smoked stuffed chicken 165
Stokbrood 167
Stuffed beef fillet 168
Stuffed pork loin chops 171
Thai mussel soup potjie 172
Tomato, bocconcini, basil and olive salad 175
Tropical prawn, pineapple and persimmon sosaties 176
Upside-down steamed pear cake 178
Vegetable sosaties 181

Acknowledgements 182

# Introduction

What sound most typifies South Africa's great outdoors? Some say it's the chilling roar of a lion in the early evening in the bush. Others claim it's the haunting call of a fish eagle that soars above the country's many rivers and dams. Still others feel it's the soft cooing of a laughing dove or the cackling of a guinea fowl coming in to roost at night.

And yet the sound that unifies South Africans all around the world is the crackling of a fire. It is the call to come together, to enjoy the hospitality so unique to our people. It is an invitation to eat together, laugh together … an invitation to share.

This book endeavours to light that fire for you, and beckons you to join us as we place a few lamb chops on the sizzling griddle and pour a glass of wine. Welcome to the great outdoors.

# Early days

So it has been since time immemorial. The sight of majestic Table Mountain is breathtaking. The lives of the folk who have settled on the southern sub-continent are simple. There are no fixed homes. No hearths. There are only the most basic of ingredients. But the weather is sublime. And a culture of outdoor cooking is already long established.

The ocean is teeming with fish. There are edible wild plants scattered along the mountain slopes, across the veld. There is wood for a fire. Indigenous groups exist entirely off the land, harvesting the fruits of the sea, trapping and hunting local widlife.

Then, in April 1652, three ships enter Table Bay, and life slowly begins to change – both for the local inhabitants and the settlers who disembark here. Outdoor cooking begins to take on a whole new meaning. Meals are now also prepared in three-legged cast-iron pots. Spices arrive from the Orient. Produce becomes more readily available. European culinary traditions begin filtering through, mingling with local custom. Flavours – and palates – start changing.

Eventually many European farmers decide to venture north, further inland, to discover what lies beyond the borders of the Cape Colony. Belongings are rationed and packed.

Three-legged pots are hung from hooks on the ox wagon and the journey begins. An animal is killed for the pot. Dried or fresh vegetables are added, if and when available.

Perhaps some starch. Every day something is added to make the meal sufficient for all.

In the evenings, the fires are stoked. When an animal is killed, some of it is cooked directly over the coals. And, like their countrymen and -women back in the colony, families eat together. They share food, laughter and the tales of the day.

# Braai

## Across the ages

What is it about a fire that we find so captivating? Can it be that it marks the time when humankind evolved and became the hunter instead of the hunted? When he found a way to protect himself, to warm himself? Well, to this day a fire is universally bewitching, perhaps because it connects us to that primal instinct within all of us.

Cooking over an open flame dates back to the very origins of fire, especially the controlled use of fire. It is likely that outdoor cooking – or what South Africans now refer to as the *braai* (pronounced *br-eye*) – happened by accident. Meat was perhaps dropped into a fire and then retrieved and eaten. Humans found that, not only did it taste better than raw meat, but it was easier to chew. They began dropping meat onto fires on a regular basis.

Archaeologists at Swartkrans, part of the Cradle of Humankind World Heritage Site, about 50 kilometres northwest of Johannesburg, where fossils dating back 2.3 million years have been unearthed, discovered burnt bones that date back around one million years. These provide conclusive proof that early humans learned to control fire a million years ago, and soon thereafter, the origins of a braai began taking shape. All here on our own soil.

# A day to celebrate

Today the braai forms part of South Africa's national psyche. It is so much part of who we are, of how we entertain, of our hospitality that on 24 September each year South Africans come together as a nation to commemorate Heritage Day – on this day we are encouraged to celebrate our culture and our diversity, both in beliefs and in traditions. It should come as no surprise then that this day has also been declared National Braai Day, because braaing remains a pivotal part of our heritage, a custom that unites us as a nation. On this day, the whole country, it seems, clusters around braais. Braai competitions are held and champions are declared.

A braai is ideal for entertaining – and a 'bring-'n-braai' is common. These are all about gathering together in a sociable environment, so everyone arrives with whatever they want to cook on the braai that day, along with salads and bread. The host provides a huge fire, and the day evolves into a party.

Although often superfluous to the char-grilled meat, salads – such as potato salad or a mixed green salad – and roasted vegetables may be served as an accompaniment. The meat, however, remains the main attraction. Braaing is unique in that it adds a mouth-watering smoky flavour to food.

Mealtimes around the fire are casual and convivial, and guests help themselves. Mostly, meals are enjoyed at an informally laid table, or on chairs close to the fire, plates perched on laps.

# *It's a cultural thing*

When it comes to domestic cooking, especially outdoors, cultural traditions tend to vary. While in suburban or peri-urban areas, such as townships, the spirit of enterprise – of earning a living – takes precedence over age-old customs that dictate gender roles, and both men and women set up, prepare, tend and serve food, mostly meat, from barrel and other makeshift braais.

In traditional black cultures, however, most members of the older generation are, with rare exceptions, set in their ways. It is usually the men, even patriarchs, who do the cooking, especially

when it comes to the preparation of certain animal parts, for example. Their task is not simply to prepare a meal in the conventional domestic sense, but one that has serious and centuries-old cultural significance. In Sepedi, for instance, the men cook the head of whatever animal is slaughtered, as well as the hooves; children do not, under any circumstances, eat the kidneys because those are reserved for elder women, the grand-mothers; while the uncle in the family has legitimate claims on meat from the head, hence 'Malome Maja Dihlogo' – Uncle: The One Who Eats the Heads. This monopoly over the head meat is symbolic, as the uncle can – and does – invite other men and family members to join him in the eating. Naturally – and not unlike their white countrymen in back yards across the country – this is often accompanied by traditional brew, and every village and family has a star brewer, one whom everyone knows and respects and is meta-phorically referred to as having 'a good hand'. By the same token, particular foods are also reserved for specific rituals, harvests, initia-tion and naming ceremonies, appeasement of gods, bereavements, and so on.

Occasionally, cooking duties may be split between the women and the men, depend-ing on the celebration or ceremony. In some ceremonies, even today, food preparation has to take place within the kraal, or homestead, so it is the responsibility of the men to do all the cooking, while the women braai their own meat beyond the confines of the kraal – in other words, 'outdoors'. This custom is true for most family gatherings, birthdays and other casual get-togethers, and stands, in a way, in direct contrast to white Western culture, where generally speaking, the un-spoken rule amongst mostly white South Africans is that the men do the braaing, with women relegated to the kitchen. But even here, amid all the light-hearted jostling, eti-quette dictates that one guy is in charge and the others do not interfere unless specifically called upon to do so.

What is clear, though, is that when it comes to outdoor cooking, be it traditional or contemporary, food is not just food – it has hierarchies, conventions, codes of conduct and, not surprisingly, great symbolism.

# The evolution of the traditional braai

Recent times have seen South Africans 'evolve' and begin to use state-of-the-art equipment and modern gadgets at their braai gatherings, but traditionally there was just a wood fire to provide the coals, sometimes with an auxiliary fire to supply new coals, and a braai grid. That was it.

At some point along the way, 44-gallon drum-halves were mounted on legs, usually welded, but their bulk, weight and size meant that these were not readily portable, and so smaller more portable braais began to make their appearance. These are now an essential part of every picnic and camping kit.

An American invention has in recent years become very popular in South Africa. The Weber® kettle braai was invented in the early 1950s by a man employed by Weber Brothers Metal Works, which manufactured nautical buoys. The wise inventor had the brilliant idea to fit a metal grid into these spun metal 'bowls' and to design a cover with vents – his thinking was that this would act as protection from the elements – and so he became responsible for transforming an ordinary grill into an oven that could

now roast a whole chicken, a leg of lamb or venison, or even a turkey. Today, aluminium foil drip trays are placed below the roast for collecting the dripping fat and juices, and potatoes and vegetables can be cooked in these containers in situ. Wood chips (soaked in water) and sawdust may be scattered over the coals to impart a smoky flavour to dishes such as chicken and fish. The Weber® is a one-stop meal-preparation device that remains the world's best-selling charcoal grill. So sophisticated has using a Weber® become that special recipe books have been developed listing, for example, the exact quantity of charcoal needed for a specific weight of meat, and a failed braai is almost impossible.

Gas braais provide instant heat and, although the meat does not have the same flavour that wood would impart, they have become very popular. Conveniently, they are portable – but, deep down, most South Africans consider gas braais a cheat!

A number of contemporary South African homes now also have built-in braais. These can be quite basic or ultra sophisticated, with adjustable shelves for heat regulation and even a rotisserie. These built-in braais may be in a sheltered area of the garden or patio or even under a roof for protection from wind, heat, rain and whatever calamity nature brings … because, come hail or high water, South Africans will braai!

# Fuel for thought

Wood was the original fuel for braaing and is still the most popular component of a good fire. Although some time is needed for the wood to burn to coals, purists believe that nothing beats the flavour imparted to meat by a wood fire. Hard woods that produce long-lasting coals are the best – such as camel thorn, rooikrans, mopane and leadwood.

In coastal regions with inconvenient rain-fall patterns, finding dry wood is often difficult so people revert to charcoal or briquettes (nuggets of compressed charcoal). The benefit of charcoal is that it can reach very high temperatures within 15 minutes, but the downside is that, once these temperatures have been reached, they lose heat rapidly.

Briquettes, though, are uniform in shape and this enables you to create a smooth bed of coals devoid of the irregular shapes of charcoal that can leave gaps in the fire. Briquettes can burn as hot as charcoal and, if correctly handled, retain heat for longer than charcoal.

In recent years, the South African authorities have initiated a drive towards the removal and eradication of invasive tree species, so you can feel quite self-righteous about burning wood. Ready-cut bags of wood can be purchased along the roadside, at fuel stations, supermarkets and convenience stores.

There are a few who choose to use gas, although a died-in-the-wool traditional braai master will deny even the existence of such heresy. The heat is instant and, as a result, gas has proven to be a convenient method when you want to barbecue but don't have the the luxury of time that a traditional wood-fired braai demands.

So what is best to use? Opinions differ. This is determined on a trial-and-error basis until each braaier is satisfied with his choice. As with most things, there are pros and cons to every approach. At the end of the day, it all comes down to a matter of personal preference.

# Enter the braai master

South African braai aficionados can be divided simply into three camps, and many are expert at more than one of these approaches.

• The traditionalist is generally something of a purist who uses only wood that is allowed to burn down to coals before any cooking is commenced. Hard woods, such as camel thorn, are favoured because of the longevity of the glowing coals that result. This purist also generally scorns the use of paraffin-based fire lighters, preferring to use natural kindling, starting with *fyn houtjies* (twigs and thin branches), slowly increasing in thickness up to the main logs.

• A product of more recent technology, the kettle-braai devotee enjoys the best of both worlds. A kettle braai can host an open fire over which meat can be cooked in the traditional way, but it is also uniquely suitable, because of its convection capabilities, for roasting whole birds, such as chicken and turkey, or larger cuts of meat, such as pork belly or leg of lamb, in a closed, succulence-preserving, oven-like environment. This approach favours the use of prefabricated briquettes or charcoal, and ignition is via synthetic fire lighters, often in conjunction with the metal chimney.

• Thirdly, is the gas braaier. Generally frowned upon by the purists, gas braais have grown in popularity in recent years, owing to the convenience of near-instant heat and an absence of the ash and smoke associated with more traditional fires.

# Essential tools

Every braaier has a few essential tools, while the more serious ones have a few extra nice-to-haves:
• a good pair of tongs – top of the list – that is long enough to avoid scorching the fingers
• a grid that clips closed to contain the meat
• a torch, for braaing at night
• a long-handled basting brush with natural bristles to keep the meat moist using the marinade
• oven gloves for handling metal skewers
• matches or a gas lighter with a long nozzle
• a drip tray if cooking in a kettle braai
• a wire brush for scouring clean the grid
• a spade for moving coals
• a stainless steel or galvanised metal chimney in which to store charcoal and briquettes
• a fish grid that clips closed and can hold a whole fish.

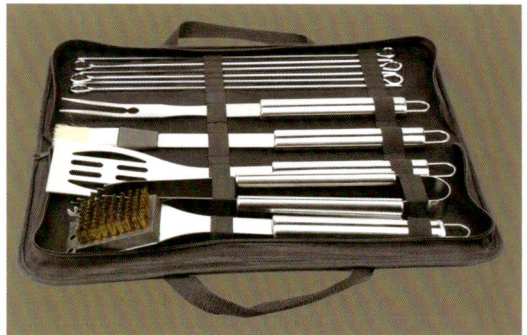

# It's all in the technique

Flavour, tenderness, whether the meat is succulent and mouth-watering or dry and overdone, it all depends on the braaier's approach – and that all-important choice of technique.

## Directly over the coals

This is what is most commonly considered 'braaing'. Here the meat is is placed directly over the coals, and is cooked faster than any of the other methods. The fire needs to be carefully watched because dripping fat will cause the flames to flare up and char the meat.

## Indirect cooking

This takes place in a covered braai and would be used for foods, such as a leg of venison, that require a longer cooking time. A foil tray is placed below the meat, and the coals are placed on either side of that. When braaing pork or duck, for example, where the meat releases a lot of fat, potatoes can be placed in the foil tray, along with herbs and an entire bulb of garlic.

# Smoking

This technique, for which you have to have a kettle braai, has become an increasingly popular way of preparing food. Wood chips, sawdust or even rooibos tea can be used. Wood chips should be soaked in water for an hour before using so that they smoulder slowly. Sawdust can be used as is, while rooibos tea is best used in small quantities in contained smokers or it could prove an expensive endeavour. Smoking in a kettle braai is best suited for something like a whole chicken, which requires a longer cooking time.

# Spitbraai

Cooking a roast on a spit (a pointed metal rod on which a piece of meat is speared) is a method that owes its success to the regular and constant rotation of the spit. It comprises two phases: the first starts at a high heat to seal the outside and ensure succulence; this is followed by a lower heat and requires a skilled operator who regularly bastes the meat with the drippings so that the inside cooks to a flavourful tenderness without scorching the outside. Meat can be roasted either horizontally or vertically. Traditionally a spitbraai involves a whole lamb or a suckling pig. Often a tray is placed below the meat and filled with potatoes or vegetables that cook in the dripping juices of the meat.

# Rotisserie

This is a battery-powered rotating spit designed for kettle braais to roast meat, such as whole chickens and whole, rolled pork bellies, in an oven-like environment. Like the spitbraai, the heat starts high and then reduces during the cooking process. This is particularly important in the case of pork belly to ensure a crisp and blistered crackling. The skin of a chicken done this way results in an inviting, evenly golden-brown colour. As with the spitbraai, most of the fat drips out, cutting the richness of the final product, but the meat remains succulent.

A spitbraai demands attention and patience, but the results are ambrosial.

# Cooking times

It is very important to experiment with different temperatures because appearances can be deceptive. A charred chicken thigh does not necessarily mean that it has cooked through – it could simply mean that the fire was too hot when the chicken was placed over the coals, or that the sugar in the marinade ingredients has burnt. So it is important to become acquainted with your braai, and to take various factors into account when determining cooking times. These may include:

• the ambient temperature
• the presence or absence of wind
• the temperaure of the meat when it was placed on the braai
• how hot the coals are at the start of a braai
• the thickness of the cut of meat
• how the meat is enjoyed – in other words, rare, medium-rare, medium or well done.

Here are a few tips on achieving perfection:
• whole chicken cooked in a covered kettle braai at between 150 and 200° C: 1 hour 15 minutes
• chicken portions cooked on an open fire at 150° C, turned frequently: about 45 minutes
• whole turkey cooked in a covered kettle braai at 200° C: 1 hour 45 minutes.

• lamb chops cooked on a medium, open fire about 2½ centimetres thick: about 10 minutes
• steak, at a thickness of about 2½ centimetres, and cooked on a hot, open fire to medium rare: 15 minutes
• deboned leg of lamb cooked in a covered kettle braai at about 180° C: about 1 hour.

preference. A young lamb will be more tender and therefore need less time on the braai, while an older animal is best done slowly at a lower temperature.

To check whether the meat is done, here are a few tips:

• The texture of meat changes during the cooking process. For a rare result, when pressed gently with a fingertip on the thickest part, the meat should feel soft. As the heat penetrates the cut, the meat becomes firmer.

• Fish is considered cooked as soon as the flesh begins to flake. It should be opaque but still moist. Overcooking fish will result in a rubbery texture.

• Chicken is tricky, but it is critical that it be cooked through. The best way to check is to use a sharp knife to cut a slit in the thick meat close to the bone, such as around the thigh joint. The meat should not be pink around the bone.

Another factor that will influence the time needed to complete the cooking process is the age of the animal and whether the meat has been matured. For example, a freshly slaughtered cut of beef will not be as tender as a well-matured cut. The latter will also need a shorter cooking time, depending on

# Braaing dos and don'ts

- Develop a relationship with a good butcher who will advise you about different cuts of meat, how long they have been aged, and how you should cook them.
- Make sure that the grill is clean before lighting up.
- Most folk have their own preferences, but the thickness of the meat will influence the cooking time and the cooking method.
- Meat from a young animal is generally more tender and requires a shorter cooking time. In the case of lamb, it can also be served pink, whereas pork and chicken, for example, need to be cooked through.
- Always allow meat to settle to room temperature before cooking. Cold, refrigerated meat will take longer to cook.
- It is always a good idea to have a side fire going in case you need to supplement the coals on your braai.
- It is not advisable to poke the meat with a fork while it is cooking. When the meat is punctured, juices will escape and the meat will be dry.
- Do not leave meat unattended on the grill. Dripping fat causes the flames to flare up and these will scorch the meat.
- When using a kettle braai, do not lift the lid too often because the heat will escape and the oven effect will be lost – and sufficient heat will have to be built up all over again.
- A crowded grill means that the meat will require a longer cooking period. Ensure that the individual portions do not touch so that the heat can penetrate from all sides.
- Do not turn the meat too frequently.

# What do we braai?

Different cultural groups have different preferences, but in general the following is what the widest spectrum of braaing South Africans like.

## Boerewors

The legacy of *boerewors* ('farmer's sausage) is one left by the German immigrants who settled here from the late 1700s onward. Today this local 'delicacy' remains the subject of much discussion and many a competition – once a year one of the largest retail groups hosts a competition to crown South Africa's boerewors champion. Contestants from every small corner of the country enter their own secret recipes, ever hopeful of winning, along with the exposure and glory that accompany this event and the grand title.

Boerewors can be found in thick and thin versions, made with a mixture of beef, lamb or pork, and a delicate or robust fusion of spices, depending on taste. Dried coriander seeds feature high on the list of ingredients.

South Africans enjoy what we call a *boerie* roll, a hotdog roll cut in half with a portion of boerewors in the middle and a choice of condiments, such as caramelised onion, tomato-and-onion *smoor* (braised tomato and onion), tomato sauce, mustard and/or chutney. The smell of boerewors cooking on the coals is one of the smells you can count on at public gatherings.

## Lamb

Lamb chops, whether loin, rib or chump, are probably the firm favourite to cook on a braai. Large stretches of South Africa lend themselves to farming with sheep, and this has led to a nation of lovers of lamb meat. Some folk will mix up a marinade for the chops, while others may simply salt it while on the grid. Lamb can be served pink, or if preferred, well done, although the latter is never as tasty or as succulent.

# marinade for lamb

For 12 chops

## METHOD

• Mix all the ingredients together and place the chops in the marinade, cover and set aside for about 1 hour.

• Turn the chops to allow the other side to marinate for another hour before grilling over the coals.

• Baste the chops with the marinade while braaing.

• This marinade also works well for a butterflied deboned leg of lamb and for *ribbetjie* (whole lamb rib) or individually cut ribs.

## INGREDIENTS

125 ml olive oil

4 cloves garlic, peeled and crushed

2 sprigs rosemary (about 10 cm long), leaves stripped from the stalks

juice of 2 lemons

One approach that might not be very traditional, but that works really well with loin or rib chops, is to line the chops up in the same direction and secure them through the middle of the chop using two skewers, all facing the same way so that the row of chops resembles an undismantled rack of lamb. Start by placing the short T-section bone close to the coals. The bone heats up and helps with the cooking process. Next the longest concave side, and by the time these two sides are cooked, the fire would have cooled sufficiently to place the fat side over the coals. The fat must cook through and crisp up, but the flames will flare up, so watch the fire carefully at this stage and keep turning the meat, still on the skewers, so that the fat doesn't scorch the meat. When the three sides have browned, remove them from the skewers and cook them briefly on the two flat sides until browned. The chops will be succulent on the inside and crisp on the outside.

## Beef

Cuts of beef, such as T-bone, rump, sirloin, rib-eye or fillet, remain popular. Fillet can be done whole or in individually cut medallions. Beef should be well aged – at least 21 days – and either wet or dry aged.

Beef requires a hot fire that will sear the meat on all sides and keep the juices inside.

Because beef, unlike lamb, tends to be drier, it is best served rare or medium-rare and should be eaten straight off the braai.

Cuts with fat on one of the sides, such as rump or sirloin, should ideally be turned intermittently onto that side in order to allow the fat to crisp up.

# Pork

Pork can be dry, so braai cuts that contain fat, such as rashers, belly and neck steaks. Sweet basting compliments pork perfectly.

For the perfect crackling, remove the belly from the container and allow to sit on a board so that the skin dries out for an hour or two. Then all you need is coarse salt (no oil) and a very hot fire. It is advisable to end the cooking process on a rising heat, so add a few (about six) white-hot briquettes 10 minutes before the cooking time is up.

Other cuts, such as chops, fillet and even smoked Kassler chops, are sometimes used, although fattier cuts remain the best.

# chicken marinade

## INGREDIENTS

250 ml brown vinegar
250 ml sunflower oil
1 tbsp salt
2 tsp coarsely grated onion
1½ tsp mustard powder
4 tbsp tomato sauce
1 tbsp Worcestershire sauce
1 tbsp Tabasco sauce
2 tsp chopped garlic
12 chicken pieces, such as
drumsticks and thighs

## METHOD

• Mix the brown vinegar, oil, salt, onion, mustard powder, tomato sauce, Worcestershire sauce, Tabasco sauce and garlic together.
• Place the chicken pieces in a dish and pour the marinade over. Set aside to marinate for at least 2 hours – preferably more. Rotate the portions periodically.
• Cook over medium coals, and baste with the marinade every time you turn the pieces over on the grid.
• Grill for about 45 minutes, on a cooler fire, rotating frequently to ensure that the skin does not char.

The skin might look charred, but this is because of the sugar in the marinade.

# Chicken

Spatchcock or butterflied chicken is popular on a braai menu. It is often referred to as a 'flattie' and can be purchased vacuum packed in a marinade. Again, a cooler fire is advisable.

Another interesting approach, when cooking a whole bird in a kettle braai, is to pour a bottle of beer into the drip tray below the meat. The beer causes steam, which rises and keeps the meat succulent. A can of beer is also often opened and inserted into the bird's cavity – the chicken then 'sits' vertically on the grill and again the beer vapour permeates the meat from inside and imparts an interesting, malty flavour.

Chicken pieces can be parboiled and then marinated.

## Duck

Duck breasts done on the grid are a treat. Because they have a relatively thick layer of fat beneath the skin, these remain succulent even when cooked on a fire. It works well to score the fat, season and cook until the fat is browned and crisp. Use a hot fire, as for beef fillet – preferably a two-zone fire in a kettle braai so there is an area where there are no coals and where the meat can cook through slightly without scorching. Duck is best served pink inside.

## Game

Game meat has traditionally ended up in pies and stews, occasionally as roasts, but seldom on the braai. However, if done properly, game done over the coals is exquisite. It is necessary to devise a plan to keep the meat succulent, however, because game – a healthier alternative to other meat – contains very little fat and can be very dry. To start, it is best served rare and thinly carved.

More so with game than any other meat, it is important to marinate the meat. As sweet flavours are the perfect compliment to game meat, a marinade containing fruit juice works really well. For the same reason, sweet jellies, like cranberry or quince jelly, are great served with game. Marinating game for a few hours and preparing it over an open fire is one of the best ways to enjoy game meat.

## Skilpadjies

*Skilpadjies* ('small tortoises') are small chunks (about 7 cm x 3 cm) of liver wrapped in *netvet* (caul fat), the fatty membrane that surrounds the kidneys and resembles a net. These should be cooked slowly on a moderate fire, allowing the fat to both drain and crisp without flame. Although rich, these bite-sized treats are a wonderful addition to a braai and delicious to nibble on while the main act is being cooked.

## Sosaties

The idea for *sosaties* (kebabs) are Dutch in origin, but like most Dutch recipes, they were enhanced by the Malay people at the Cape. The word *sosatie* comes from *sate* (the modern Indonesian spelling of 'satay') and *saus* (spicy sauce). They are cubes of meat, usually lamb, traditionally marinated in a sweet curry marinade, skewered and cooked on a fire. Because of the Malay influence and their preference of combining sweet and spicy, the meat chunks are interspersed with a choice of small onions, sliced peppers, mushrooms, dried apricots or dried prunes.

For maximum flavour, sosaties should be marinated for 24 hours. Although lamb is traditional, beef, pork, chicken and vegetable sosaties are also popular. In fact, a vegetable sosatie is a great way to include vegetarians at a braai.

Sosaties should be cooked over a moderately hot bed of coals and turned a few times until they are cooked on all sides. Remember to ensure that all the ingredients are cut into equal-sized portions so that they cook evenly.

# Breads

• *Roosterkoek* (griddle cakes) are easy to prepare. All you need is the dough, a grid and a fire. The yeasted dough balls should be cooked on a relatively cool fire – to test if the coals have cooled down sufficiently, you should be able to hold your hand over the coals for 10 seconds without it being unbearable. If the fire is too hot, the roosterkoek will scorch on the outside while still raw on the inside. Traditional toppings for roosterkoek include farm butter, apricot jam and grated cheese, but like all traditions, this too has evolved and can now be served as breakfast rolls topped with scrambled egg, tomato and bacon, while toppings such as brie and caramelised onion are perfectly acceptable too.

• *Stokbrood* (bread on a stick) is a fun activity for kids, because it keeps them at a safe distance from the fire. Bread dough is wrapped around a long stick and held over the fire to cook slowly.

• *Braaibroodjies* (braaied sandwiches), essentially toasted tomato-and-onion *sarmies* (sandwiches), are a tried-and-tested favourite at braais. White bread is a prerequisite, although brown bread can be used, and the sandwiches are filled with slices of onion and ripe, fragrant tomatoes, and seasoned with salt and white pepper. In this instance, a light scraping of butter goes on the outside surfaces of the bread. Adding grated cheese, such as cheddar, is a later addition that has enhanced the humble sandwich even further. These, like roosterkoek, are also cooked over cooler coals until they are a rich, golden brown on both sides, and should be served hot off the grid. This being said, there is nothing nicer than a cold braaibroodjie for breakfast the next day!

# roosterkoek

Makes 10 to 12

## METHOD

• Dissolve the dry yeast and honey in about 1 cup of the luke-warm water. Stir 1 tablespoon of the flour into this mixture, cover and leave in a draught-free spot for 5 to 10 minutes to activate.

• Sift the remaining flour and salt into a mixing bowl. Make a hollow and add the yeast mixture. Mix and knead well until the dough is smooth. Add as much water as is needed gradually while kneading. Knead the soft butter into the mixture until evenly distributed.

• Cover with a dishtowel and place in a warm spot to rise to double its size. Then knock it back and form balls of about 4 cm in diameter. Place these on a lightly floured breadboard and flatten them a little. Cover with the dishtowel again and allow to rise a little before placing the rolls on the grid.

• Place over coals of medium heat so as not to burn them on the outside too quickly. Turn regularly until browned on both sides.

• Serve hot with butter, cheese and an assortment of jams.

## INGREDIENTS

2 tsp dry yeast
2 tsp honey
750 ml lukewarm water
1 kg all-purpose flour
1 tsp salt
1 tbsp butter, at room temperature

Farm butter, apricot jam and grated cheese make great toppings.

## Fish

If you're intending to braai fish, be sure to choose a firm-fleshed variety such as snoek (a local fish resembling a barracuda), yellowtail or Cape salmon. It is best to keep the skin on the fish. The fish should be cleaned and prepared, the fresher the better, and then cooked whole, either butterflied or closed (fish cutlets are likely to flake and fall off the grid). For this, a special fish grid comes in handy. As fish flakes and breaks easily, the grid clips closed and keeps the fish intact. The grid is then turned with the fish inside, which also makes serving so much easier.

Traditionally, snoek – which can be quite dry – is basted with a mixture of butter and smooth apricot jam while on the fire. Smaller, more oily fish, such as galjoen and mackerel, are best placed on the grid whole, with slices of lemon, a dab of butter, salt and pepper to season, and either rosemary, basil or tarragon spread on the inside. This method works well for yellowtail, steenbras, Cape salmon and kabeljou as well.

Fish should not be cooked for too long on the braai, so be sure to check it as as soon as the skin has browned on a moderate fire, using two forks to part the flesh. As soon as the flesh has flaked, the fish should be removed and enjoyed.

## Lobster

The meat of the lobster – known locally as *kreef* – is delicate, both in colour and flavour. It is best enjoyed in a simple way that will enhance the flavour. To prepare lobster is quick, easy and very simple. All that needs to be done before it is cooked, is to cut open the underside of the tail to remove the dark, thin entrails. Rinse the lobster in fresh seawater and it is ready to be prepared.

There are two ways to cook lobster. You can either bring a big pot of seawater to the boil on the open fire, and when boiling vigorously, place the whole lobsters in the pot and replace the lid. They should be ready within 7 minutes.

Or, you can braai them. To do so, it is advisable to cut the lobster in half lengthways, keeping it in its shell, and removing the entrails. A sturdy pair of kitchen scissors works well for this purpose. Rinse the lobsters in fresh seawater. Place them over hot coals, shell side down, and baste regularly with a mixture of melted butter, fresh crushed garlic, chopped parsley and freshly squeezed lemon juice. The basting is absorbed into the flesh and adds flavour.

Lobster really needs very little time to cook and it is ready to be eaten as soon as the flesh turns white. It can be eaten either warm or cold, but is really delectable when eaten straight off the grid.

## Prawns

Prawns are also easy and quick to prepare, and like crayfish, need their entrails to be removed before cooking. Uncooked prawns are either charcoal, light grey or light pink in colour, and turn a bright pink when cooked.

While cooking, they should be kept in their shells and basted with a mixture of melted butter, fresh lemon juice, crushed fresh garlic and chopped parsley, and are best eaten straight from the braai.

# Potjiekos

## Introducing the three-legged pot

Cast-iron cauldrons date back to the Iron Age when humans learnt to cast iron into vessels and into different shapes for different purposes. These played an essential role in homes in medieval Europe and were used over indoor hearths as well as outdoors over a fire.

Most of the original cauldrons had round bellies and were ideal for suspending over coals. Because the only way to regulate heat distribution was to change the height of the pot in relation to the fire, meals were simple and limited in variety.

When the early explorers left the old world and set sail for the new world that beckoned, the cast-iron pot was an integral part of their impedimenta. Away from home and hearth, very often they had no choice but to prepare meals over an open fire. Wherever they stopped for the day, women had to cope with make-do open-air kitchens. Suddenly there was a new problem to face – how to keep the round-bottomed pot from toppling over. So, like most innovations, the cast-iron pot underwent an evolution and soon the three-legged version, with its rounded lid, appeared – ideal for steady cooking over an open fire.

Not only did this invention serve people from around the world, but it became essential to the expeditions into the interior of southern Africa. It wasn't long before rural African communities spotted these vessels and, seeing how useful they were, began trading them for animal hides and other sought-after commodities. These cast-iron pots soon replaced the clay pots that had been using for cooking until then.

Among the indigenous people these pots became known as *putu* pots (*putu* being the maize porridge that was their staple food). Today the *potjie* (pronounced *poy-key*), as it now commonly referred to locally, is used extensively by almost all the cultures that call this land home. Once the legs had been added, the potjie shape remained unchanged over the centuries simply because it is so practical. This age-old invention has lived to tell the tale!

*Potjiekos* ('pot food') has the war between the Netherlands and Spain from 1566 to 1648 to thank for its origins. At the time and under those circumstances, food was scarce and people were forced to eat what the Dutch called *hutspot* (hodgepodge) to survive. Folk contributed what they could, adding whatever meagre morsels they had at home. These were added to a large communal pot and cooked together. People shared. Not long after this war, the Dutch brought this idea to Africa.

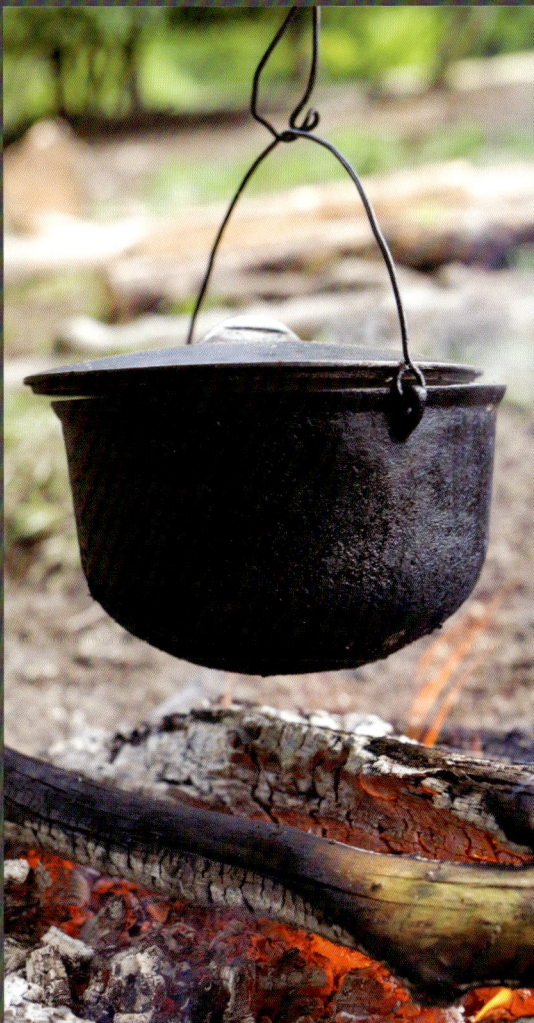

The early settlers used these pots not only for cooking potjiekos, but also for baking bread utilising the potjie as an oven, always over an open fire. When the trade route between Europe and the East was opened, spices and herbs became more readily available and these contributed to the evolution of potjiekos, one of South Africa's oldest and most significant food traditions.

This method of cooking is an economical way of feeding families that suited the nomadic lifestyle of both the indigenous communities and the *Voortrekkers* (pioneers) in the seventeenth and eighteenth centuries. To thicken the gravy, the Voortrekkers added the large bones of hunted animals to the pot and each day, when the wagons stopped to rest, a fire was made and the pot placed back on it, perhaps with the meat of a newly hunted animal added to what was already there. Flavours were absorbed into the pores of the cast iron, and released when heated, and today's bones and meat replaced what had been eaten the day before. Meat included guinea fowl, various francolin species, hare, warthog and bush pig.

# Dos and don'ts of potjies

Today all potjiekos champions, whether self-proclaimed or having earned their stripes, have their own secrets to ensure gourmet success. There are, however, a few pointers that will contribute to the enjoyment of the final result:

• To prevent rusting, used potjies should always be protected by a thin layer of fat or oil after they have been cleaned.

• Because of the convection effect of these pots, very little liquid is needed. Always cook covered so that enough liquid forms from the condensation of the steam and juices.

• The lid, necessarily heavy and rounded, should be lifted as seldom as possible because this allows the steam to escape. A good way to gauge whether any extra liquid is needed is by listening for a gentle bubbling, which is the sound of a healthy potjie. If the pot cooks dry during the cooking process, liquid will need to be added, a little at a time, so as not to lower the temperature.

• Always start by heating a little oil in the bottom of the pot and frying the meat and onion in that until browned. The flavour of the caramelised onions and the braised meat are the building blocks from which the gravy is created.

• Because the pot is made from cast iron and has a rounded belly, it heats up evenly all round and retains this distributed heat very well.

• You do not need a huge fire and prolific flames – in fact, these are counter-productive. Constant small flames, from burning sticks on a bed of hot coals, should be enough to keep the fire going.

• It is best not to leave your pot unattended because, although the heat must remain low, it must also be constant – attentive stewarding is essential.

• As soon as the meat has cooked for some time and a liquid has formed, vegetables are layered on top of the meat. Start with those that take longer to cook, such as potatoes and carrots. As more time passes, add the vegetables that need less time and allow them all to steam.

• The main difference between potjiekos and a stew is that the latter is stirred and all the flavours in the pot mingle while the objective of potjiekos is to try to keep the flavour of all the ingredients separate by leaving them in their individual layers during the cooking process.

• Typical timing for a potjie is anything between 3 and 6 hours, depending on the size of the pot – and the amount of beer imbibed by the chef.

Potjiekos is all about the flavour and requires attention; and because it needs to be tended for hours, it also fascilitates social interaction. In essence, it can bring together a great group of friends, a lazy afternoon, a good bottle of wine or a cold beer, a fire, the promise of a great meal, much laughter, and delectable aromas.

## Other uses for cast-iron pots

Flat-bottomed cast-iron pots are used for baking potbrood (pot bread). To bake bread golden brown, the pot has to be lifted off the coals to a varying degree, depending on how fierce the heat is. Small coals are placed on the lid and the bread rises and bakes to perfection.

# Fish and seafood

Fish is an important part of the diet of many South Africans. Not only is the country hugged on three sides by an ocean – the Atlantic on the western coastline and the Indian on the eastern coastline – but the map of our landscape is sliced into sections by the almost 300 watercourses, varying in size from streams to large rivers. Many dams are also dotted across the land, all of which offer great potential for both sea and fresh-water fish.

The two oceans are responsible for a steady supply of fish and seafood – the colder Atlantic Ocean supplies mussels, oysters, West Coast rock lobster, abalone and an array of fish species, such as snoek, yellowtail and Cape salmon, while the warmer Indian ocean is responsible for prawns, East Coast rock lobster, calamari and fish species such as shad.

One remarkable difference between the two oceans can be seen in the colour of the fish. Fish in the warmer Indian Ocean are bright and often multicoloured – the colours aid with predator evasion. On the opposite side of the spectrum, sluggish species in the colder water are mostly brown and yellow in colour.

# Kosi Bay fish traps

Early fishing methods, such as trapping, were much more sustainable than they are today and therefore minimised the impact on fish populations. One excellent example is the traditional trapping method, most conspicuous at Kosi Bay.

Kosi Bay, South Africa's first World Heritage Site, is a series of four interlinked lakes in KwaZulu-Natal, close to the Mozambique border. These lakes drain, via a sandy estuary, into the Indian Ocean. Kosi is also the cultural capital of the ancient Tsonga Tembe Kingdom and the Tsonga people have occupied this land for more than 1000 years.

For centuries, the local populations have been trapping fish in huge, woven, basket-like structures, which are built in waist-deep water and handed down from generation to generation. No bait is needed because the fish are guided along a curved palisade, made from reeds, that resembles a hook – they swim into one or more circular pens called *kraals*. Once a fish has entered through a specially designed gate, the larger fish cannot escape and are trapped. Once a day, the trap owner checks his kraals and spears the fish that arrived overnight.

## The ancient fish traps of Stilbaai

In the little coastal town of Stilbaai (literally 'quiet bay'), not far from Agulhas, and close to the famous Blombos archeological site, ancient fish traps, dating back up to 3000 years, are still being used today.

Fish traps were the easiest way for people from the Stone Age to catch fish, and these were built by the indigenous Khoisan. They were mostly in a half-moon shape and varied in size. They came about through the careful observation by cave dwellers, who noticed that fish became trapped in natural pools as the tide receded. To catch more fish, logically, they needed to enlarge these pools. So they began strategically packing stones to form artificial tidal pools. On dark nights the fish, oblivious of the receding tide, were trapped in the pools and could be caught by hand.

Creating and maintaining these *vywers* (weirs) as they are known, is an ancient art known to only a few. The side of the pool facing the ocean must have a gentle slope to enable the fish to swim into the trap. The internal walls are vertical and clear of debris to enable fast draining. In recent years the introduction of nets have made it easier to catch the fish trapped in the pools.

Traditionally, guardianship over a vywer was handed from father to son, but in recent years the owners have formed a corporation and the catch is now divided amongst the families. Ponds were given names and more than 20 are still maintained and in use. A number of the locals work together to ensure that this tradition remains alive. The best time to see these ponds in action is during the winter months.

## Fishing using plant poisons

Hunter-gatherers have used fish-stupefying plants for ages. Various local species can be used. The tamboti flourishes along rivers and streams in the northern parts of South Africa. It secretes a milky latex that is poisonous to humans. However, this substance is successfully used in isolated river pools that contain fish. It stuns the fish, and they then float to the surface and are thus easily retrieved. Because the poison affects the functioning of the gills and does not contaminate the rest of the fish, the flesh can be eaten without ill effects. Other species that can be used include the naboom, a succulent plant indigenous to southern Africa.

## Cast nets

A cast net is a woven, circular net with small weights secured around the edge. Throwing these nets in a way that they spread out on the surface of the water before sinking is an arcane skill that has been in use for thousands of years. The nets are then closed and retrieved by pulling on a handline attached to one end and held in the hand when the net is thrown.

Cast nets work best in shallower water and are good for catching smaller species, such as sardines and harders (mullet), which form shoals. The harders are often salted and dried and sold as *bokkoms*.

# Saltwater fishing today

Oceans have traditionally been regarded as a limitless source of seafood, when, in fact, the supply is indeed finite. South Africa is no different. For centuries the ocean has provided us with sometimes invisible social, cultural and economic benefits. It has facilitated a highway for commerce of all kinds, it provides recreation, and most importantly has provided an income and sustenance for the people of this land.

Sadly, however, the ancient tradition of fishing, transmuted by modern technology into an act of plunder, has in some cases depleted fish stocks to dangerous levels and has tipped the balance of a fragile ecosystem to such an extent that the existence of a number of key species is threatened. According to recent statistics, many fish species that were commonplace in South Africa in the 1950s and 1960s have now become endangered. SASSI (South African Sustainable Seafood Initiative) plays a significant role in monitoring these levels and providing information to educate consumers about the role they can play, however small, to help restore the balance.

With the country's coastline at around 3000 kilometres, fishing plays an important role in the lives of many of South Africa's people. Fisheries influence the livelihood of many, and fish is a critical source of protein for people from traditional fishing communities along our shoreline. Squid fishing in the impoverished Eastern Cape region, for example, is this country's most financially viable form of marine export.

## Line fishing

Line fishing is both a relaxing and sociable pastime – amateur and small-scale professional fishermen line up along harbour walls or on long beaches to catch something for the pot, but also to catch up with others. Commercial boats also practise line fishing.

Unfortunately, much of South Africa's coastline has been overfished, and although the main culprits are fishing trawlers, this phenomenon can be controlled if minimum size standards are adhered to, threatened species are released, and the environment is not polluted with synthetic line debris. Fortunately, on the other hand, commercial fisheries are carefully regulated by law to protect the oceans from overfishing.

# Deep-sea fishing

From many points along the country's extensive coastline, sport fishermen sally forth, usually at an insanely early hour, and travel considerable distances out to sea in pursuit of the elusive 'big one.' The various fish species that frequent deep waters are the quarry, with sushi-grade tuna probably topping the list. Other species include marlin, swordfish, snoek and yellowtail. All are caught on a line and make for exciting fishing.

# The flavour spectrum

| Mildly flavoured fish | Medium-flavoured fish | Intensely flavoured fish |
| --- | --- | --- |
| • angelfish<br>• cob (kabeljou)<br>• shad (elf)<br>• hake<br>• kingklip<br>• sole | • musselcracker<br>• dorado<br>• Cape salmon (geelbek)<br>• gurnard<br>• mullet (harder)<br>• sea bream (hottentot)<br>• monkfish<br>• red roman<br>• red snapper<br>• red steenbras<br>• silverfish<br>• stumpnose<br>• swordfish | • butterfish<br>• horse mackerel (maasbanker)<br>• marlin<br>• sardine<br>• snoek<br>• tuna<br>• yellowtail |

## Recreational shallow-water diving

Because so many fish species have become endangered, recreational diving is not permitted in marine conservation, protected and closed areas. Careful monitoring is enforced by government and permits are essential for the harvesting of any of the following and other species: shellfish such as *perlemoen* (abalone), wild oysters and *alikreukel* (giant periwinkle or sea snail).

Also monitored by law, but still a popular pastime (you will need to apply for an official permit), is catching rock lobster, especially in hoop nets from a boat. Lobsters hang around in shallow water around rocks and kelp, and the West Coast variety is the largest of the species in South African waters. Under-sized lobsters must be released.

Lobster on the braai, or in a curry, or, quite honestly, done any which way, is very popular and a real treat.

# Freshwater fly-fishing

In keeping with the custom of transferring their own species to all corners of the Empire, British colonists introduced trout, both rainbow and brown, to the cooler mountainous areas around South Africa in the late 1800s. Both species require cold water conditions and can thus be found in some of the most picturesque valleys and breathtakingly beautiful parts of this country – from the rivers below the majestic Drakensberg, the valleys just outside Cape Town and to the dams of Mpumalanga, there is something for everyone.

The art of flyfishing was initially developed as an angling method to catch salmon and trout. And although, years ago, it was mainly enjoyed by older folk, it is a sport that is fast catching on with the younger generation. Flyfishing, however, is not only an art, but a skill: the angler has to cast the fly gently above the water, taking care not to touch the surface – in so doing, alarming the fish – and put it down artfully, mimicking the soft landing of an insect. The resulting rhythmic movements of the angler's rod and line, swishing forward and

backward, slowly gaining length, in the quiet ambience of a stream of running water is both soothing and a marvel to behold. The trout, being a predator, will then dash towards the 'insect' and so get hooked.

The intricate art of fly tying is practised by many enthusiasts, and provides anglers with particular joy to know that a big fish was caught on one of their own flies. Studying the insect life on and around the water gives anglers a very good idea of what the fish are feeding on, and at what time of day. To try to emulate this by tying lookalike flies is half of the joy of fishing.

Brown trout are a challenge. They are very wary and have selective feeding habits. They are also scarcer and can only be found in select spots in KwaZulu-Natal, the Eastern Cape and Western Cape. Larger fish are predominantly nocturnal and prefer to feed in the late afternoon or early evening. They tend to be more solitary and territorial, which makes finding them so much more of a challenge.

Rainbow trout are more plentiful in our rivers and dams and are also widely farmed. Delicacies such as hot-smoked and cold-smoked trout, generally from farmed rainbows, are plentiful on our shelves

Although fly-fishing on our rivers is mostly on a catch-and-release basis, trout makes for good eating. Other freshwater fish, such as catfish, bass, carp and yellowfish, tend to be bonier than their saltwater cousins. There is also the chance of a muddy taste. They, therefore, have to be prepared correctly, and if done properly, provide a great source of protein to many.

So how does one eliminate the 'muddy' taste from freshwater fish? This flavour is caused by the presence of two chemicals that accumulate in dirty parts of the river. So start by catching fish in clean, rapid-flowing waterways. And, when preparing the fish, soak the fish in milk for at least an hour before cooking. These two methods should eliminate the taste of mud in the fish.

# Hunting and venison

Although most South Africans today are focused on conservation and ethical hunting practices, hunting has always been, and still is, part of the national psyche. Africans across the continent have of course depended on hunting for survival since time immemorial but, at the time of the arrival of the early European settlers, hunting in the northern hemisphere was a sport reserved for the nobility, so those arriving on these shores knew very little about hunting and their weapons were inadequate. But game was plentiful here and hunting soon became a popular pastime of the high-ranking officers and later of most men. In fact, game meat was a regular feature on local menus.

Lord Charles Somerset, governor of the Cape in the mid-1800s, was such a keen hunter that he built the first hunting lodge on the slopes of Lion's Head in Cape Town, above Camps Bay. The building has since been renovated and utilised as a restaurant.

## Shooting for the pot

Hunting for venison for the pot is an age-old ritual that possibly began as a way of defence against wild animals, and soon progressed to a source of sustenance that spoke to humankind's need for survival. Certainly in the mid-1600s, when the Cape was colonised, hunting with a rifle was already a way of life. Commander Jan van Riebeeck wrote in his journal that they had to shoot wild animals that were trashing their fledgling vegetable garden. Later, when it became clear that bartering for livestock with the indigenous people would be harder than expected, the settlers turned to game for an additional source of protein.

Although there has been a recent trend toward bow hunting, which requires great skill and is an art that takes both time and patience to perfect, rifles are still the most commonly used hunting firearm. In the Western Cape, for instance, there has been a resurgence of wingshooting targeting the local pigeon populations – even for the pot – a pastime that has been likened to shooting driven grouse in the British Isles. Much the same is true in parts of

the Free State, where marksmen shoot pigeons and game birds, such as helmeted guinea fowl, when they come in to feed on the sunflowers. In the Southern Drakensberg and Stormberg areas, the principal habitat for greywing francolin, hunters walk the top of the mountain at around 9000 feet above sea level, depending on their trusted gun dogs to help them. The various pointer species locate the birds, the hunter walks in and flushes the birds, shoots, and relies on a retrievers to fetch the bird.

Preparing game birds for the pot and cooking them is quite an art form that is not widely practised. Most game birds tend to be dry and are best prepared in a stew or a pie. Duck and geese are also abundant in the country and many, though not all, make for good eating if skilfully prepared. This is an arena of wing-shooting where a good retriever really earns his keep. There is also open season on other spurfowl and francolin species in various parts of the country.

Preparing game birds requires some care. They fall into two categories – those that can be plucked and those that need to be skinned. Eating a guinea fowl that has not been skinned is a little like eating a chocolate bar with the wrapper still on. The same applies to wild geese. When the bird is shot, the entrails, including the crop, should be removed, as well as the neck, head, wings and tail feathers. Birds that need to be skinned include guinea fowl and wild geese. To skin the bird, a slit is made, using kitchen scissors, from the belly upwards, and the skin, along with the feathers, is peeled off like one would remove a cardigan. Birds that are best plucked include pigeons, francolin, spurfowl, wild duck and quail. Game birds should be kept refrigerated for five to seven days for the meat to tenderise.

Antelope species such as springbok, gemsbok, kudu, duiker (literally meaning 'diver', named after the diving motion it makes when running), steenbok, eland, red hartebeest and both species of wildebeest are popular when it comes to eating. Traditionally, game was most commonly served as pie, using an array of spices introduced from the Orient that helped mask the wild flavour. However, although game pies are still popular, today game meat is enjoyed on the braai, as steaks and as whole roasts.

Fallow deer introduced into the country have thrived, and also make for good eating, but smaller game species, such as warthog, bush pig, porcupine and wild hare can also be delectable additions to a menu and can be cooked in a number of different styles.

To ensure ultimate tenderness, three factors are critical when it comes to reparing and cooking venison in any form:

• The animal needs to be shot skilfully and cleanly so that adrenalin is not given the chance to course through the system and toughen the flesh.

• The meat should be hung in a cool, dry area for long enough (this depends on ambient conditions) to allow enzyme activity to tenderise the meat.

• A good marinade is invaluable in combating the inherent tendency of venison to become dry.

As with any meat, as a general principle, care should be taken to remove all sinews and fascia (thin sheets of fibrous covering certain muscles). Fruit (either fresh or dried), fruit jellies, and fruit juice enhance the flavours of any venison dish. Venison is a healthy alternative to beef, lamb and pork.

# Variations on the theme

South Africans are known to be a creative bunch, and even to come up with ingenious plans of their own – especially when it comes to livening up their menu. The following are a few local variations on outdoor cooking.

## Gat hoender

*Gat hoender* (loosely translated as 'hole chicken') is chicken cooked in a hole in the sand that is used as an oven. A hole, about half a metre deep, is dug in the sand, a thick layer of hot coals is placed at the bottom and a whole chicken, seasoned and spiced, with garlic, quartered onions and chunks of carrot, is wrapped in a few layers of thick aluminium foil is placed on the coals. Then more coals are placed on top of the foil package before the hole is covered over with the sand and left for a few hours. As soon as the chicken is retrieved from the hole and the foil is unwrapped, an appetising aroma escapes and the meat falls off the bone.

## Termite ovens

Early on, in the 1800s when the Voortrekkers were moving inland, they began to use hollowed-out termite heaps, built taller than normal ant heaps, as ovens in which to bake bread. This gave rise to the phenomenon of an outdoor oven, amply provided by nature. The lower portion of the heap is hollowed out and filled with wood, which is lit and burnt down to coals. The walls are insulated and retain the heat for long enough to be useful for cooking.

## Fish in newspaper

Cooking trout in newspaper is something South Africans inherited from the English. To do this, clean the fish, rinse and pat it dry. Place the fish on about 10 sheets of newspaper, and season. At this point, you can choose to add Oriental flavours such as lemongrass, ginger, red chillies, lime, kaffir lime leaves and coriander, or simply add slices of lemon and some tarragon. Drizzle with olive oil, wrap in the paper and secure the parcel with string. The trout parcel is then soaked for about five minutes in water, and as soon as the coals on the fire have turned white, and are therefore very hot, it is placed on the grid, and turned occasionally. When the paper has dried out and has become scorched, the fish will be ready. Unwrap and enjoy.

## Klip rib

Lamb ribs are fatty and tricky to braai because the dripping fat causes flames to flare up. But, when cooked between two rocks (*klip* means 'rock' in Afrikaans), the fat mostly burns off. Place three large, grit-free, flat, igneous (fire-resistant) rocks, on top of each other, in the fire to heat up for at least an hour. Taking great care – the rocks will be very hot – sandwich the seasoned ribs between two of the rocks, leaving them in the fire. Should the top rock cool too quickly, you may need the third rock to complete the process. After 45 minutes, lift the rock, remove the ribs and cut into portions.

## Veggies in the coals

Potatoes and onions cooked in the coals are a delicious treat. The outside scorches and the inside of both go creamy. The potatoes will have a nutty flavour and the onions will be sweet and caramelised. This is a great idea when camping, and you can place the potatoes and onions in the fire after the afternoon braai, when the coals have cooled down slightly. Leave them there for a few hours, ready to be retrieved in time for dinner.

# Conclusion

It is the twenty-first century, and the old traditions of open-air cooking are still very much alive. So pull up a chair, warm your hands over the fire and savour the fragrance of the smoke. Be mesmerised by the ever-changing shape of the flames and the sound of burning wood filtering through the stillness of the outdoors, shooting its orange sparks into the night… Enjoy what we have prepared for you.

**Beware!**
Fires are permitted only in private domestic premises and in designated parts of urban areas and, no matter where one is lit, it has to be watched carefully. A small errant spark can cause extensive damage, especially if there are strong winds blowing. Also, if a fire is not thoroughly extinguished, it can reignite later, with the same disastrous consequences for the landscape and indigenous wildlife. Braai responsibly.

# recipes

# baked camembert

## INGREDIENTS

1 small round of camembert (125 g)
4 fresh dates
8 plump raspberries

## METHOD

• Place the camembert in a clean, used tuna can lined with parchment paper.
• Put to one side of the coals in a very hot kettle braai, cover the braai and bake for 15 minutes.
• Make mini sosaties using the fruit.
• When the cheese is done, cut a circle into the top of the cheese, lift the 'lid' and enjoy by dipping the fruit kebabs into the melted cheese.

Baked camembert is a great dessert to be enjoyed around the fire.

# braai broodjies

Serves 2

## METHOD

• Butter the slices of bread and turn them upside down, with the buttered sides on the outside.

• Spread a thin layer of chutney on one of the slices, then add slices of tomato and season with salt and pepper. Add slices of onion and top with grated cheese.

• Close the sandwiches and place on a small grid that clips closed so that they can be turned without the sandwiches falling apart.

• Cook on a medium-to-hot fire until golden brown on both sides.

• Remove from the fire and serve hot, with the melted cheese oozing out, with a lamb chop and boerewors.

## INGREDIENTS

butter, softened
4 slices white bread
fruit chutney
1 small tomato, sliced
salt and white pepper
1 small onion, sliced
100 g cheddar, grated

Although these are best enjoyed straight off the fire, they are equally delectable the next day.

# breakfast in a pan

Serves 6

## INGREDIENTS

3 tbsp oil
3 tbsp butter
4 to 6 large potatoes, peeled and coarsely grated
salt and freshly milled black pepper to season
handful of chives, finely chopped
generous handful of dill, finely chopped
6 eggs
100 g cold-smoked trout ribbons
2 tbsp crème fraîche
lemon wedges

## METHOD

• Heat the oil and butter in a large pan over a hot fire.
• Add the grated potato and cook for about 20 minutes until crispy – gently move the potato around to make sure it cooks evenly.
• Season and add the chives and dill. Cook for a few minutes longer.
• Using a spoon, form six hollows in the potato mixture and break an egg into each.
• Cook on a lower heat until the egg whites have set and the yolks are still runny.
• Top with the trout and more black pepper.
• Serve one potato nest per person, with blobs of crème fraîche and a wedge of lemon.

# broccoli, leek and bacon salad

Serves 4

## INGREDIENTS
500 g tender-stem broccoli
200 g bacon, cut into smaller pieces
3 medium-sized leeks, cut into slices
mayonnaise

## METHOD
• Trim about 1 cm from the browned bottoms of the broccoli and steam for 15 minutes until al dente.
• Rinse in cold water and set aside on a paper towel to dry.
• Heat a pan and fry the bacon bits until crispy. Drain on a paper towel and wipe some of the excess fat from the pan before flash frying the leeks.
• Mix together the leeks and the bacon and set aside.
• Cut the broccoli into smaller chunks, and mix in mayonnaise to coat the broccoli.
• Mix in half of the bacon-and-leek mixture. Spoon onto a platter and top with the remainder of the bacon and leeks.
• Serve as an accompaniment to smoked stuffed chicken (see page 165).

# butternut on the coals

Serves 4

## METHOD

• Lay two sheets of heavy-duty foil on the work surface and place a blob of butter on each. Place a butternut half, skin down on the blob of butter, onto the foil.

• Mix the rest of the ingredients together and scoop into the hollows of the butternut.

• Cover with the foil to form a parcel and then wrap each parcel in another layer of foil before tucking them into the coals, placing a few coals on top of each parcel as well.

• Leave for 30 to 40 minutes. Ideal as an accompaniment to game meat.

## INGREDIENTS

2 blobs of butter

1 butternut, halved lengthways and pips scooped out

3 ginger biscuits, crushed

pinch of salt

1 tbsp treacle sugar

50 g sundried cranberries

50 g salted macadamias

10 walnut halves, finely chopped

¾ tsp cinnamon

50 g butter, melted

# Cape salmon in vine leaves

## INGREDIENTS

### Marinade

250 ml olive oil
100 ml lemon juice, freshly squeezed
zest of one lemon
125 g calamata olives, pipped and sliced
2 tbsp fresh rosemary, roughly chopped
salt and freshly ground black pepper

### Parcels

6 portions of Cape salmon (about 220 g each)
Preserved vine leaves (about 300 g)

If Cape salmon is unavailable, any firm-fleshed fish can be used.

## METHOD

• To make the marinade, mix all the ingredients together and allow to infuse for 2 hours before using – store in the refrigerator until needed.
• Wrap the individual fish portions in the vine leaves, making sure that the parcels are well covered and secure.
• Place the portions in the marinade and allow the flavours to mingle for 2 hours, turning the portions once or twice during the process.
• Remove the fish from the marinade, gently scraping the olives from each portion so as not to burn over the high heat, and place securely on a grid.
• Braai over a medium-to-hot fire, basting regularly, until the leaves have browned. Milky droplets from the fish indicate that the portions are cooked through.
• Serve topped with a spoonful of the olive marinade and a salad.

The preserved vine leaves are salty enough, so no extra seasoning should be necessary.

# citrus angelfish on the braai

Serves 4

## INGREDIENTS

1 whole angelfish, head removed
2 tbsp butter
1 tsp smooth apricot jam
juice of a ¼ orange
zest of ½ an orange

## METHOD

• Score the fish on both sides.
• Melt the butter and jam together and add the juice and zest.
• Place the fish in a grid and cook over a medium-to-hot coals. Regularly baste the fish with the mixture, paying special attention to flames that may flare up due to the dripping butter.
• Check the thicker part of the flesh where the head has been removed to see whether the fish is ready. As soon as the pinkish flesh turns white and opaque, and the skin is nicely charred, the fish is ready.
• Serve with a crusty loaf and potato gratin (see page 158.

For best results be sure to source your fish fresh from a trusted fishmonger.

# curried green beans

Serves 4 to 6

## METHOD

• Chop the beans into small pieces.
• Cook the beans, onions, water and salt together for 10 minutes.
• Mix the remainder of the ingredients and add to the bean mixture. Cook until the beans are at the desired degree of softness.
• Allow to cool before refrigerating and serve cold with braaied meat.

## INGREDIENTS

500 g fine green beans, topped and tailed
1 large onion, peeled, halved and cut into slices
300 ml water
1 tsp salt
190 ml white vinegar
1½ tsp corn flour
1 tsp mild curry powder
½ tsp turmeric
200 g sugar

Traditionally South African and great with a braai.

# curried pork-neck sosaties

Makes 6

## METHOD

• To make the marinade, place the onion in a saucepan and add just enough water to cover. Cook for 5 minutes until the onions are transparent but still firm.

• Drain the water, add the butter and fry until the onions begin to brown. Then add 250 ml water and allow to simmer slowly until the onions have softened.

• In a small bowl, mix the curry powder, turmeric, cornflour, sugar, salt, vinegar and chutney and add to the onions. Cook for 3 minutes and then add the bruised lemon leaves. Set aside to cool.

• When the mixture has cooled, place the meat in a glass dish and pour the curry mixture over. Mix, coating the meat with the sauce. Cover with a lid and allow the meat to marinate for 2 to 3 days, mixing it around once a day.

• Soak sosatie sticks in water for at least 30 minutes. Skewer three pieces of meat, interspersed with two pieces of red onion and one dried peach onto each stick. Season to taste.

• Place on a grid that clips closed and cook over hot coals, basting regularly and being careful to not scorch the sosaties.

• When nicely browned, remove and serve immediately with a salad.

## INGREDIENTS

**Marinade**

2 large onions, peeled and cut into slices
25 g butter
250 ml water (plus extra for boiling onions)
2½ tsp curry powder
1 tsp turmeric
2½ tsp cornflour
5 tsp sugar
1 tsp salt
500 ml vinegar
125 ml fruit chutney
4 fresh lemon leaves, bruised

**Sosaties**

3 thickly cut pork-neck steaks, cut into 18 even chunks
1 red onion, peeled and cut into quarters
6 dried peaches, soaked in warm water
salt and white pepper to season

# dessert jaffels

Makes 1

## METHOD

• Heat the jaffel iron over the flames.

• Butter each slice of bread on the outside. Spread a layer of chocolate spread on the dry side of one of the slices, keeping to the middle of the slice. Add the slices of banana and top with the marshmallows.

• Close the sandwich and place into the heated jaffel iron and clip shut. Trim off the excess bread and discard.

• Hold over the flames, turning occasionally, until golden brown on both sides.

• Serve hot with a steaming cup of coffee.

## INGREDIENTS

2 slices white bread
butter, softened
chocolate spread
½ banana, sliced into discs
4 marshmallows

A sweet treat to enjoy while sitting around the fire.

# flambéed plums

## INGREDIENTS

2 tbsp butter
8 to 10 plums, halved and pips removed
1 tsp vanilla essence
3 tbsp yellow sugar
a good glug of brandy
125 ml cream

## METHOD

• Melt the butter in a pan over hot coals. Place the plum halves in the butter and cook on both sides until softened. Then add the vanilla essence and sugar. Cook until the sugar has dissolved.
• Place the pan over the open flames and add the brandy. Tilt the pan so that the brandy burns off.
• Serve hot with cream.

A sweet ending to a braai.

# four-cheese pap bake

Serves 6 to 8

## METHOD

- Preheat the oven to 180° C.

- Add the water to the mealie meal in a heavy-based saucepan, then add the salt and gently bring to the boil, stirring constantly to avoid lumping. Reduce the heat and allow the pap to bubble away, stirring occasionally, for 40 minutes.

- Stir the butter into the mixture, and pour into a shallow casserole about halfway up the sides of the dish, and about 4 to 5 cm thick. Leave to cool completely while you prepare the sauce.

- For the sauce, heat the oil in a saucepan and fry the onions until they begin to brown. Add the garlic and continue frying lightly.

- Add the chopped tomato, oregano, salt and pepper, and allow to gently simmer for another 20 minutes before adding the sugar. Remove from the heat and set aside.

- When the pap is cold and set, turn it out onto a wooden board. Use a sharp knife to slice it in two horizontally, so that you have two 'sheets'. Pour half of the tomato sauce into the bottom of the casserole dish. Top with one of the sheets of pap.

- Scatter the Gorgonzola and Emmentaler over and dot the mascarpone on top. Sprinkle half the Parmesan onto the other cheeses and top with the second sheet of pap.

- Top the dish with the remainder of the sauce and the Parmesan and bake for 30 minutes.

## INGREDIENTS

### Pap
300 g mealie meal
1.5 litres water
2 tsp salt
75 g butter

### Sauce
3 tbsp olive oil
2 medium-sized onions, chopped
2 large cloves garlic, crushed
400 g can chopped tomato
1 tbsp oregano, chopped
1 tsp salt
freshly milled black pepper to taste
1 tsp sugar

### Filling
50 g mascarpone
100 g Gorgonzola
150 g Emmentaler, grated
100 g Parmesan, finely grated

# garlic-and-herb potbrood

Makes 1 loaf

## METHOD

• Mix all the dry ingredients – the flour, yeast, sugar and salt – in a bowl. Make a hollow in the middle and add the olive oil and water. Mix to form a dough – you might need to dust a little extra flour. Knead the dough for a few minutes until smooth and elastic. Place in a lightly oiled bowl, cover with plastic wrap and a dishtowel and allow to rise in a warm spot until it has doubled in size.

• Melt the butter and mix into the herbs. Set aside to cool.

• Punch down the dough and press into a rectangular shape on a lightly floured surface.

• Spread the herby butter mixture onto the top of the dough and roll into a rough sausage shape. Twist and bring the two ends together and secure. Place in a lightly buttered flat-bottomed potjie.

• Brush the bulb of garlic with butter and press into the centre of the bread. Place the lightly buttered lid on top, cover with a dishtowel and leave to rise for 30 minutes.

• Move a layer of coals to one side while keeping the flames going on the other side to supplement the coals later. Place the pot on top of two bricks, which have been turned onto their sides for extra lift, over the bed of coals. Place a row of smaller, hot coals on top of and around the rim of the lid for a crisp crust.

• Bake for 1½ hours, supplementing coals regularly to make sure the temperature remains even. To test if the bread is done, tap the loaf – it should sound hollow.

## INGREDIENTS

4 cups cake flour
20 g instant dry yeast
1 tsp sugar
1 tsp salt
2 tbsp olive oil
2 cups warm water
50 g butter (plus extra to brush the inside of the pot and the garlic)
2 tbsp chives, finely chopped
2 tbsp parsley, finely chopped
2 tbsp thyme, finely chopped
1 whole bulb of garlic

If baking this in an oven in the potjie with a lid, bake for 50 to 60 minutes.

# hamburgers

Serves 6

## INGREDIENTS

### Patties

4 slices stale white bread, crusts removed and softened in water
400 g lean lamb mince
1 large clove garlic, crushed
1 medium-sized onion, finely chopped
8 tbsp chives, finely chopped
2 tbsp flat-leaf parsley, finely chopped
½ tsp nutmeg
salt and pepper to season
olive oil

### Burgers

6 hamburger rolls
butter
1 tomato, sliced
1 small red onion, sliced
iceberg lettuce

## METHOD

• Squeeze the water from the bread and then mix all the patty ingredients, except the olive oil, in a large bowl until well combined. Divide the mince mixture into 6 balls and form patties by pressing them flat to the size of a small saucer and about 2 cm in thickness. Rub each with olive oil and set aside.

• When the coals are ready – they should be hot – place the patties on a grid and braai until browned on both sides.

• Butter the rolls and place them briefly on the braai to brown.

• Place some iceberg lettuce, topped with slices of red onion and tomato, and a patty on each before serving.

Mayonnaise, tomato sauce and mustard make great additions to a simple hamburger.

# honey-and-mustard chicken thighs

Serves 6

## METHOD

- Soak 24 sosatie sticks in water for 1 hour.
- Mix the honey, mustard and lemon juice in a bowl.
- Spear the thighs crossways using two sticks per thigh, and place in a flat dish.
- Pour the honey-and-mustard mixture over and allow the chicken to marinate for 1 hour before cooking on medium-hot coals until golden and sticky.

## INGREDIENTS

2 tbsp honey
6 tsp wholegrain mustard
juice of ½ lemon
12 deboned chicken thighs

Sticky, tangy and most enjoyable.

# mango, fennel and lobster salad

## INGREDIENTS

4 large lobster tails (in the shells)
50 g butter, melted
juice of ½ a lemon

### Salad

2 ripe mangoes, peeled and cut into thin slices
1 fennel bulb, shaved
125 ml mayonnaise
pomegranate arils

## METHOD

• Use a serrated knife to make a cut in the bottom side of the shell of the lobster tails.

• Braai the tails on a medium-to-hot fire, turning regularly and basting the opened side with the butter. Squeeze lemon juice over the tails. As soon as the flesh turns opaque, the tails are ready. Remove from the heat and allow to cool.

• To assemble the salad, break the lobster tails open and remove the entrails. Keep the tails whole and intact.

• Serve one tail per person, with mango slices, shaved fennel and 2 tablespoonfuls of mayonnaise. If desired, more mayonnaise can be used. Top with pomegranate arils and some fennel leaves.

• Serve at room temperature as a refreshing starter.

Lobster doesn't take long to cook. When it is removed from the heat as soon as it is done and served immediately, lobster meat is a real treat – but when overcooked, it can be rubbery and less pleasant.

# marinated springbok

For 1 deboned leg or backstrap

**METHOD**

• Mix the oil, apricot juice, wine, lemon juice, garlic and rosemary together.

• Place the meat in a dish and pour the marinade over. Marinate for at least 4 hours, even overnight, turning the meat occasionally.

• Remove the meat from the marinade and allow to drain. Then, using a flour shaker, liberally coat the entire cut with a layer of flour, which will form a crust that seals the meat and keeps it succulent.

• While on the grid, continually baste with the remainder of the marinade, and shake flour onto the meat every time it is turned. (The last dredging of flour should take place no less than 10 minutes before the meat is removed from the fire or the flour will remained uncooked.)

• Season with salt and pepper at the last minute.

**INGREDIENTS**

250 ml canola oil
250 ml apricot juice
250 ml dry white wine
juice of 2 lemons
4 cloves garlic, chopped
4 sprigs rosemary, leaves lightly bruised
1 deboned leg of game (about 1½ kg)
flour in a flour shaker
salt and pepper to season

Game meat is a healthy alternative.
Serve immediately to avoid the meat drying out.

# marrow bones

## INGREDIENTS

6 thick marrow bones
drizzle of olive oil
coarse salt
6 sprigs rosemary

## METHOD

• Fold a sheet of aluminium foil into three, folding the sides up slightly to form a sturdy holder.
• Place the marrow bones onto the foil, drizzle with a little olive oil and some coarse salt. Push a sturdy sprig of rosemary into the marrow of each bone.
• Place in a hot kettle braai and cook with the lid on until brown and crispy.

Serve with a hot, crusty loaf.

# mealie bread in a can

Bakes 2 loaves in 410 g cans

## METHOD

• Spray two clean, used food cans with non-stick spray and preheat the oven to 170° C.

• Mix the eggs, salt, butter and milk in a bowl and then stir the flour and spring onions into the mixture and combine.

• Pour the mixture into the cans and bake for 30 to 40 minutes until golden brown.

• Remove from the cans and allow to cool on a cooling rack.

## INGREDIENTS

410 g can creamed sweetcorn
2 eggs, lightly beaten
1 tsp salt
30 g butter
60 ml milk, warmed
350 g self-raising flour
2 spring onions, finely chopped

ow, Zapiro
mean. I think Mbalula meant that
those sports are, metaphorically, the
big game, and Zapiro treated it in a
-high-school glee. Rather shallow.
Zapiro's usual acidity.
Walt, by e-mail
into power.
If the DA comes
because a black guy
A politician is only as
influence, his followers. The
many years undefeated
re not yet ready to
to the election
going into

# mealies on the coals

Serves 4

METHOD

• Place the mealies on a small grill over a hot fire, basting regularly with the butter mixture.

• Cook until the kernels begin to brown. Serve hot.

INGREDIENTS

4 mealie cobs, with leaves intact
80 g butter, melted
handful flat-leaf parsley, chopped

## Serve with extra butter and sea salt flakes.

# mushroom risotto

## INGREDIENTS

25 g dried porcini mushrooms
1 cup warm water
1 tbsp butter
2 tbsp olive oil
120 g shitake mushrooms, roughly chopped
150 g shimeji mushrooms, roughly chopped

### Risotto

2 tbsp olive oil
2 tbsp butter
½ onion, very finely chopped
2 cloves garlic, crushed
1 cup Arborio rice
3 tbsp chives, finely chopped
1 tbsp thyme, finely chopped
30 ml dry vermouth (or white wine)
2 to 3 cups vegetable stock
75 g Parmesan, finely grated
1 tbsp parsley, finely chopped
zest of 1 lemon

## METHOD

• Soak the dried porcini mushrooms in warm water for at least 30 minutes.

• Heat the butter and oil in a skillet and cook the fresh shitake and shimeji mushrooms over the fire. When they begin to brown, squeeze the water from the porcini and add to the skillet. Cook for a few more minutes and then set aside.

• To make the risotto, heat half the butter and the oil in a flat-bottomed, cast-iron pot. Add the onion and garlic and cook over a very low heat until both are transparent.

• Add the rice and increase the heat so that the rice fries in the onion mixture for about 5 minutes. Then add the herbs and fry for another minute.

• While the onion-and-rice mixture is frying, lightly heat the vermouth and stock seperately. Then add the vermouth to the rice and stir until absorbed.

• Start to ladle the stock into the pot, one ladle at a time, stirring between each addition until the liquid has been absorbed before adding the next. Continue adding the stock until the rice is just al dente.

• Fold the cooked mushrooms into the risotto. Then stir in the Parmesan and remaining butter. Allow to rest for a few minutes.

• Serve topped with extra Parmesan, chopped parsley and lemon zest. If using unsalted stock, seasoning might be required.

# old-fashioned potato salad

Serves 6

## METHOD

• Cover the potatoes with water, add salt and boil for 15 minutes or until soft. Set aside to cool.

• Mix the mayonnaise, mustard, honey, onion and parsley together.

• When the potatoes have cooled, remove the peels and add to the mayonnaise mixture, mix and serve with lamb chops from the braai.

## INGREDIENTS

30 baby potatoes

1 tbsp salt

1½ cups mayonnaise

2 tbsp wholegrain mustard

2 tsp honey

1 small red onion, peeled and chopped (not too finely)

2 good handfuls of flat-leaf parsley, chopped

A firm favourite at every braai.

# oxtail-and-orange potjie

Serves 6

## INGREDIENTS

3 tbsp olive oil
500 g oxtail, excess fat trimmed
2 large onions, peeled and cut into eighths
3 cloves garlic, peeled
4 cardamom pods
400 g can peeled and chopped tomatoes
250 ml red jerepigo
250 ml orange juice
3 large carrots, peeled and cut into chunks
salt and pepper to season
zest of 1 orange

## METHOD

• Heat the oil in a potjie over a hot bed of coals with some smaller pieces of flaming wood. Brown the meat and add the onion so that it also browns.

• Add the garlic and cardamom and cook for 3 minutes before adding the tomato, jerepigo, orange juice and carrot chunks. Cover and cook at a gentle simmer for 3 hours – refrain from stirring the pot often. The cooking process requires small flames under the pot.

• The meat should be falling off the bone – if not, there is no harm in cooking it for longer.

• Serve with basmati rice or *krummelpap* (crumbly pap).

# pizza with red onion, parsley and Parmesan

## INGREDIENTS

### Base

1 tbsp caster sugar
2 tsp dried yeast
215 ml lukewarm water
450 g all-purpose flour
½ tsp salt
3 tbsp olive oil

### Topping

olive oil
1 red onion, very thinly sliced
2 generous handfuls flat-leaf parsley, chopped
150 g Parmesan, finely grated

This pizza base is like an blank canvas and you can play with colours and toppings. Anything goes, from a tomato-and-mozzarella base, topped with other savoury ingredients, to a Nutella base with various sweet toppings.

## METHOD

• For the base, place the sugar and yeast in a small bowl and stir 90 ml of the lukewarm water into the mixture. Leave to activate in a draught-free spot. If it does not bubble and foam within 5 minutes, discard and start again.

• Mix the flour and salt in a bowl. Add the olive oil, the remaining 125 ml lukewarm water and the yeast mixture. Mix until it clumps together. Kneed for 8 minutes – add a few drops of water if needed – until a soft dough forms.

• Rub the dough with olive oil and cover with plastic and then a cloth and leave in a draught-free spot for between 60 to 90 minutes until the dough doubles in size.

• Punch the dough down and divide into six balls. Roll the balls out, one at a time, and brush the top with olive oil.

• Top the pizza by sprinkling the onion slices, parsley and Parmesan over the top, leaving about 2 cm clear around the edges.

• Place on a heated pizza stone in a covered kettle braai at a temperature of around 400° C. Bake until brown around the edges, and serve hot.

# pork trotters and beer potjie

Serves 8

## INGREDIENTS

3 tbsp olive oil
1.5 kg pork trotters
8 small pickling onions, peeled but left whole and with bottoms intact
1 stick cinnamon
3 large sage leaves
440 ml draught beer
salt and pepper to season
10 baby potatoes, peeled
3 tsp apple jelly
1 tsp wholegrain mustard
425 g can preserved baby apples, drained

## METHOD

• Heat the oil in a potjie and brown the pork and the onions. Add the cinnamon, sage and beer and season to taste. Simmer for 1½ hours with the lid on, without stirring the pot too often.

• Lift the lid and tuck the baby potatoes into the juices. Simmer for another 30 minutes.

• Heat the jelly until liquid and then mix in the mustard before pouring into the pot. Give the pot a gentle stir and add the baby apples.

• Heat through and serve with basmati rice.

# potato gratin in a pot

Serves 6

## INGREDIENTS

4 large potatoes, peeled and cut into very thin slices
generous sprinkling of nutmeg
salt and pepper to season
250 ml cream
handful of chives, finely chopped
30 g Parmesan, finely grated

## METHOD

• Place a few blobs of butter in the bottom of the pot. Arrange the potato slices in circles around the bottom of the pot so that they overlap slightly. Repeat until all the slices have been used.

• Sprinkle the nutmeg over the top and season with salt and pepper. Pour over the cream and top with the chives and cheese.

• Cover with the lid and cook over a bed of coals, with coals placed all along the rim of the pot lid too. Cook until the potatoes are soft.

• Serve as an accompaniment to meat.

Because this dish is cooked in a closed pot, steam forms inside, which adds more liquid to the pot. When the potatoes are beginning soften, remove the lid to allow some of the liquid to cook off.

# quince jelly

Makes about 3 x 250 ml jars

## METHOD

• Wash the fruit and rub off the excess fluff using a paper towel.

• Chop the fruit into chunks, skin, pips and all. Place in a pot and cover with water.

Bring to the boil. As soon as the mixture begins to boil, lower the heat to a slow but steady simmer and cook for 45 minutes to 1 hour until the fruit is soft and mushy. If the water level drops during this process, add more water to cover the fruit.

• Ladle the mixture into a muslin cloth and suspend over a deep bowl to allow the liquid to drain overnight.

• The next day, discard what's left in the cloth. Measure the strained liquid and pour this back into a pot. Add an equal quantity of sugar, the lemon juice and the rose water.

• Cook over a high heat, stirring gently until the sugar has dissolved. Bring to the boil and allow to bubble away briskly for 30 minutes. A white foamy scum will appear on the surface – use a spoon to skim this off the top. As the mixture bubbles it will become clear and turn a light maroon colour.

• To test whether the mixture is ready, drop a teaspoonful onto a cold granite surface and allow to rest for 1 to 2 minutes. If it becomes wobbly, it is ready.

• Skim off any residual scum and ladle into sterilised jars. Seal while hot and set aside to cool.

## INGREDIENTS

6 quinces
white granulated sugar
water
juice of 2 lemons
2 tbsp rose water

Quinces take on a rose-petal scent when cooked, so the rose water enhances this. This jelly can be stored for up to a year, and is great served with game, such as springbok (see page 143).

# smoked stuffed chicken

Serves 4 to 6

## METHOD

• To make the stuffing, cook the Arborio rice in the stock until tender and the liquid has dried up.

• Melt the butter in a saucepan and fry the onion until it begins to caramelise. Add the nuts, raisins and garlic, and fry for a few minutes before adding the muscadel and tarragon. Combine well and set aside to cool.

• Place the whole chicken on a board and stuff the rice mixture into the cavity. Secure the stuffing by using toothpicks to pull the skin over the cavity.

• Rub the chicken with olive oil and season both sides.

• Prepare the kettle braai with two beds of briquettes on either side of a drip tray. Place the chicken over the drip tray at around 350° C and cover. Cook for 1 hour 15 minutes. Lift the lid after 15 to 20 minutes and sprinkle sawdust on each bed of coals before covering the kettle braai again. Do this about four times during the cooking process.

• When the time's up, the bird will be browned and crispy on the outside, while succulent inside. Serve immediately.

## INGREDIENTS

½ cup Arborio rice
1 cup chicken stock
2 tbsp butter
1 medium-size onion, peeled and chopped
handful pistachios, shelled
handful crimson raisins
1 clove garlic, peeled and crushed
2 tbsp muscadel
handful chopped tarragon
1 whole chicken
olive oil
salt and freshly milled pepper

Sawdust is usually available in the braai section at local supermarkets. You can also use oak shavings.

# stokbrood

Makes 4 to 6

## METHOD

- Mix the honey, melted butter, warm milk and egg together. Add the dry ingredients and mix to form a dough. Knead for a few minutes until smooth and silky.
- Cover with a dishtowel and leave in a warm, draught-free spot to double in size.
- Punch back the dough and divide into four to six even balls. Roll out each ball into a long sausage shape.
- Using a non-toxic stick thick enough to hold the dough, wrap the sausage shape around the stick in a tight spiral.
- Cook over medium to hot coals until brown and cooked. Serve with honey.

## INGREDIENTS

1 tbsp honey
2 tbsp butter, melted
100 ml milk, warmed
1 egg, lightly beaten
1 packet (10 g) active dry yeast
1 tsp salt
500 g all-purpose flour

To test whether the bread is properly baked through, it should sound hollow when tapped. The hollow that is left when the stick is removed can be stuffed with cheese or boerewors for a variation on the theme.

This is a fun activity for children because the stick keeps them at arm's length from the fire.

# stuffed beef fillet

Serves 4 to 6

## INGREDIENTS

2 tsp chives, finely chopped
120 g sundried tomato in olive oil, drained and chopped
1 wheel of feta, crumbled
800 g beef fillet
olive oil
salt and pepper

## METHOD

• Mix the chives, sundried tomatoes and feta together.
• Cut a slice in the top part of the fillet, about two-thirds of the way into the meat. Stuff the mixture into the pocket and secure the meat using toothpicks. Rub the fillet with olive oil.
• Braai over hot coals, beginning on the side of the filling, browning each side before turning. Season with salt and pepper.
• When browned, remove from the fire and allow to rest for a few minutes.
• Cut into slices of about 2 cm thick and serve with potato gratin (see page 160).

To prevent the filling from dropping out, handle the meat as little as possible while it is on the fire.

# stuffed pork loin chops

Serves 4

## METHOD

• Heat a pan and fry the bacon and onion until browned – the bacon has enough fat so no extra oil is needed. Allow to cool.

• Mix the bacon and onion with the cheddar, corn and chives.

• Using a sharp knife, cut pockets into each chop, starting opposite the bone and cutting to quite close to the bone.

• Stuff the pockets with the filling and secure with toothpicks.

• Braai over medium-to-hot coals, turning carefully to keep the filling inside.

• Once the chops have browned on both sides, remove from the coals and season with salt and pepper. Remove the toothpicks and serve.

## INGREDIENTS

150 g bacon, cut into small pieces
1 small onion, finely chopped
100 g cheddar cheese, finely grated
100 g whole-kernel corn
handful of chives, finely chopped
4 thick-cut pork loin chops, 'crackling' removed
salt and pepper to season

Pork loin can be quite dry and is best served immediately after removing from the heat, before it dries out further.

# Thai mussel soup potjie

## INGREDIENTS

250 g fresh mussels
1 tbsp coconut oil
2 cloves garlic, peeled and crushed
thumb-sized piece of fresh ginger, peeled and grated
1 tbsp grated lemongrass
1 red chilli, pipped and finely sliced
3 spring onion, chopped
1 tsp tamarind paste
2 tsp fish sauce
2 tsp ponzu sauce
280 g can baby clams
400 ml coconut milk
juice of ½ a lemon
1 cup stock (from steamed mussels)
80 g rice noodles

## METHOD

• Steam the mussels over water. As soon as they open, remove from the heat and set aside to cool, retaining the liquid over which the mushrooms have been steamed. Once they have cooled, remove the beards and leave them in the shells.

• Heat the coconut oil in a potjie. Add the garlic, ginger, lemongrass and chilli and fry for the flavours to be released. As soon as the garlic has turned transparent, add the spring onions, tamarind, fish sauce, ponzu sauce and baby clams, along with the liquid in the tin of clams.

• Heat the mixture through before adding the coconut milk, the lemon juice and the mussel stock.

• Bring to the boil and add the rice noodles. Cook until they have softened, and serve.

# tomato, bocconcini, basil and olive salad

Serves 6

## METHOD

- Place the tomatoes, bocconcini and olives in a bowl.
- Tear the basil leaves and add.
- Season and dress with the olive oil and lemon juice.
- Serve with braaied lamb chops.

## INGREDIENTS

500 g mixed baby tomatoes, halved
200 g bocconcini
100 g green olives, drained
100 g black olives, drained
fresh basil
coarse salt and freshly milled black pepper
olive oil
juice from a ¼ lemon

Bocconcini are small mozzarella balls and are available at most supermarkets.

# tropical prawn, pineapple and persimmon sosaties

Serves 4 as a starter

## INGREDIENTS

1 whole pineapple, peeled and cut into chunks (about 3 x 3 cm)
12 fresh prawns in their shells
1 persimmon, cut into quarters
2 tbsp coconut oil
1 tbsp chopped mint

## METHOD

• Soak 4 sosatic sticks in water for 30 minutes.
• Skewer a chunk of pineapple onto each stick, followed by a prawn, a quarter of persimmon, another prawn, pineapple chunk, and then the final prawn.
• Melt the coconut oil and add the mint.
• Cook the sosaties on a hot fire, basting them with the coconut oil mixture – but make sure that the oil doesn't cause the flames to flare up.
• As soon as the prawn meat turns opaque, the sosaties are ready.
• Serve hot with a final basting of the coconut and mint.

The persimmon can be substituted with pipped, canned litchis.

# upside-down steamed pear cake

## INGREDIENTS

2 heaped tbsp honey
2 heaped tbsp treacle sugar
1 can pear halves
100 g butter, softened
100 g caster sugar
120 ml pear juice (from the canned pears)
240 g cake flour
2 tsp baking powder
pinch of salt
2 heaped tsp ground mixed spice
Greek yoghurt

## METHOD

• Place a round of parchment paper on the base of a flat-bottomed cast-iron pot and lightly butter the paper and sides.

• Heat the honey and treacle sugar in a small saucepan until the sugar has dissolved. Then pour the sugar-and-honey mixture onto the paper in the pot.

• Cut the pear halves into slices and arrange around the base of the pot.

• Beat the softened butter and caster sugar together until light and fluffy. Add the juice from the canned pears, followed by the flour, baking powder, salt and mixed spice. Mix well.

• Spoon the mixture over the pears and place the pot over the coals. Position a few coals on the lid of the pot and cook for about 40 minutes. Then remove the lid and cook for another 10 minutes. Allow to cool for about 10 minutes.

• Once cooled, flip the pot over onto a serving plate and remove the parchment paper.

• Serve warm with thick Greek yoghurt.

# vegetable sosaties

Makes 8

## INGREDIENTS

2 red peppers, pips removed and cut into chunks
4 red onions, peeled and cut into quarters
8 cauliflower florets
8 yellow patty pans
8 white mushrooms
8 baby aubergines, topped
4 jalapeño chillies, pips removed and cut in half
olive oil
2 cloves garlic, peeled and crushed
coarse salt

## METHOD

• Soak sosatie sticks in water for at least 30 minutes.
• Skewer the red pepper, followed by the onion, cauliflower, patty pan, mushroom and baby aubergine. End with the chilli.
• Mix the olive oil and the garlic in a small bowl.
• Grill the sosaties on a bed of hot coals and baste regularly with the olive oil mixture, making sure that they don't scorch in the flames caused by the dripping oil. Season with the coarse salt.
• When the vegetables are chargrilled, remove from the fire and serve.

Other than the chillies, ensure that the vegetables are cut quite uniform in size.

# Acknowledgements

**The following were a great help and inspiration in writing this book:**

- Hilary Biller, Elinor Storkey and Jenny Kay, *Braai* (Struik, 2008)
- Matthew Drennan, *Weber®'s Ultimate Barbecue Book* (MQ Publications Ltd., 2001)
- Megan Emmett and Sean Pattrick, *Game Ranger in Your Backpack* by (Briza Publications, 2010)
- www.braai.com
- Stilbaai Tourism
- Kosi Bay Tourism
- www.wwf.org.za
- www.wwfsassi.co.za
- WOSA (Wines of South Africa),*Cape Wine Braai Masters*

Special thanks to:
- Paddy Lindop
- Dalene Kapah
- Neil Austen
- Tinus Lamprecht
- Debbie Wieland
- Dawid Rossouw
- Nico Traut
- Sean and Tracey Fraser of PHRASEworks
- Jacana Media

Photography:
Sophia Lindop, with contributions from:
Hougaard Malan: pp. 2–3, 4–5, 8–9, 14, 17, 29, 40, 64, 69, 83, 101, 102, 105, 107; Tinus Lamprecht: pp. 75, 76–77, 86, 97; Debbie Wieland: pp. 20–21, 25, 26, 37, 54, 63, 183; Tracey Fraser: pp. 66, 106; Dawid Rossouw: pp. 88, 90–91, 92–93, 94; Gale McAll: pp. 46, 72; Liezel Kershoff: pp. 85; Neil Austen: pp. 18–19, 60, 78, 80, 98; Nico Traut: pp. 50

First published by Jacana Media (Pty Ltd in 2015
Second impression 2017

10 Orange Street
Sunnyside
Auckland Park 2092
South Africa
(+27 11) 628-3200
www.jacana.co.za

© Text: Sophia Lindop, 2015
© Photography: Images copyrighted as credited on page 182, 2015

ISBN 978-1-4314-2201-2

Edited by Sean Fraser
Design and layout by Tracey Fraser
Set in Helvetica 9 pt
Job no. 003044
Printed and bound by Creda Communications

See a complete list of Jacana titles at www.jacana.co.za